The Proper Way to
Meet a Hedgehog
And Other How-To Poems

selected by **Paul B. Janeczko**

illustrated by **Richard Jones**

CANDLEWICK PRESS

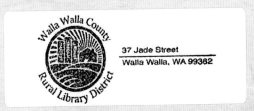

Contents

How to Build a Poem

Let's build a poem
made of rhyme
with words like ladders
we can climb,
with words that like
to take their time,

words that hammer,
words that nail,
words that saw,
words that sail,
words that whisper,
words that wail,

words that open
window   door,
words that sing,
words that soar,
words that leave us
wanting more.

CHARLES GHIGNA

How to Tell a Camel

The Dromedary has one hump,
The Bactrian has two.
It's easy to forget this rule,
So here is what to do.
Roll the first initial over
On its flat behind:
The Bactrian is different from
The Dromedary kind.

J. PATRICK LEWIS

How to Be a Mole

Make your home
in the damp darkness
underground
unknowing of snow
and stars
and summer breezes.
Live among roots
and rocks
and sleeping cicadas.
Excavate tunnels
in the moist brown earth.
Listen for the soft music
of seeds sprouting,
worms wiggling,
rain pattering on your grassy roof.
Spend your days in a world
of unending night.

ELAINE MAGLIARO

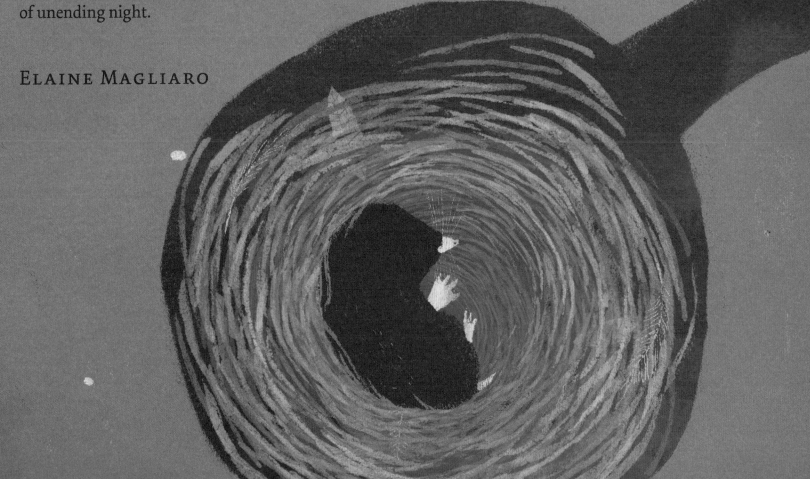

The Proper Way to Meet a Hedgehog

Today I walked outside and spied
a hedgehog on the hill.
When she and I met eye to eye,
she raised up straight and still.

The quills across her back puffed out.
She froze in blind alarm.
In turn, I ceased to move about
to show I meant no harm.

Awhile we stood there silently
in time as if to say,
"I'll leave you be if you leave me,"
then went our separate ways.

Allan Wolf

Toasting Marshmallows

It hinges on a second, an inch.
A shade too long, a hair too close,
    and perfect crisp brown
        turns to bitter charcoal,
    gentle melting
        becomes ooze.
And you lose the game,
    the marshmallow
        to the flame.

MARILYN SINGER

Mix a Pancake

Mix a pancake,

Stir a pancake,

Pop it in the pan;

Fry the pancake,

Toss the pancake—

Catch it if you can.

CHRISTINA ROSSETTI

To Make a Meal

Find yourself a water cracker.
Top it with a kipper.
Sprinkle it with pepper.
Now you have your supper.

Pick a couple custard apples.
Clean 'em with your shirt.
Place on each a slice of peach.
Now you have dessert.

CALEF BROWN

How to Tell Goblins from Elves

The Goblin has a wider mouth
    Than any wondering elf.
The saddest part of this is that
    He brings it on himself.
For hanging in a willow clump
    In baskets made of sheaves,
You may see the baby goblins
    Under coverlets of leaves.

They suck a pink and podgy foot
    (As human babies do),
And then they suck the other one,
    Until they're sucking two.
And so it is that goblins' mouths
    Keep growing very round.
So you can't mistake a goblin,
    When a goblin you have found.

MONICA SHANNON

How to Scare Monsters

Keep a light on, that's the thing.
All closets open, too.
Every fifteen minutes say:
I'm not afraid of you.

Then sharply fold a paper plane.
Fly it down the hall.
Aim for a toe (did you know this?)
They don't like that *at all*.

REBECCA KAI DOTLICH

Rules

Do not jump on ancient uncles.

Do not yell at average mice.

Do not wear a broom to breakfast.

Do not ask a snake's advice.

Do not bathe in chocolate pudding.

Do not talk to bearded bears.

Do not smoke cigars on sofas.

Do not dance on velvet chairs.

Do not take a whale to visit
Russell's mother's cousin's yacht.

And whatever else you do do
It is better you
Do not.

KARLA KUSKIN

Rules of Speaking

When speaking, you should always stand,
But not on someone else's hand.
Don't bite your nails or suck your thumb.
Refrain from saying, "Um, um, um."
Speak in a voice both clear and deep,
And cover those who fall asleep.

DOUGLAS FLORIAN

Walking on Mars

Bounce in your boots,
skip like you're six years old.

Trust your equipment.
Listen to Mission Control.

Marvel at craters.
The desert is yours to explore—

barren places invite
our imaginations to soar.

Acknowledge the power
of that fine, rusty dust.

It can blind you and bury you
when the wind starts to gust.

Don't take off your helmet,
whatever you do—

be ready:
the first person to walk on Mars

might be you.

IRENE LATHAM

Table Tennis Triolet

It's all in the spin
and the blur of the ball,
knowing how, knowing when;
that's all. In the spin,
you can grab the big win
or lose the ump's call.
Find it all in the spin
and the blur of the ball.

MARJORIE MADDOX

Basketball Rule #2

(Random text from Dad)

Hustle dig
Grind push
Run fast
Change pivot
Chase pull
Aim shoot
Work smart
Live smarter
Play hard
Practice harder

KWAME ALEXANDER

How to Ride a New Bike

Reflector?
Head protector?

    Let's ride!

Quick quiz, Cycling Whiz:
When car turns in a flash,
how won't you crash?

    Brake hard!
    Brake fast!

You won't last.
You'll fly
past handlebars
seeing stars.

Next guess?
(Less mess, please.)

    Feather brakes slow
    bike doesn't throw me
    so I touch ground
    safe and sound?

Yup. You've got guts—
A-plus!

APRIL HALPRIN WAYLAND

Playin' Jacks

shake those jacks
shake 'em, shake 'em

throw them down
on the ground

toss that ball
not too high

now pick
quick

reach and grab
ball in hand
try again

throw
thump
swipe
catch

onesies
twosies

mesies
yousies

playin' jacks
playin' jacks

ANNA E. JORDAN

The Swing

How do you like to go up in a swing,
    Up in the air so blue?
Oh, I do think it the pleasantest thing
    Ever a child can do!

Up in the air and over the wall,
    Till I can see so wide,
Rivers and trees and cattle and all
    Over the countryside—

Till I look down on the garden green,
    Down on the roof so brown—
Up in the air I go flying again,
    Up in the air and down!

ROBERT LOUIS STEVENSON

How to Bird-Watch

A Tanka

be very quiet
and amazingly patient
until finally
a shy dove thinks your green shirt
is part of a shady tree

MARGARITA ENGLE

How to Be a Tree in Winter

Enough hiding—

drop any leaves
that linger.

Etch your
message

in calligraphy

across
a parchment

sky.

IRENE LATHAM

How to Take Care of Your Tree

Hug his trunk when he's afraid
of summer hurricanes and floods.
In springtime feed him lemonade
when he begins to sprout taste buds.

In fall when you discover that
a lack of leaves has left him naked,
knit your tree a stylish hat
from all the leaves that you have rakéd.

Or use a bit of tape and glue
to reattach each leaf that fell.
It takes a while, but when you're through,
your tree will be so grateful.

When winter winds begin to blow
and snowdrifts rise up higher and higher,
wrap your tree in calico
and keep him warm with Mom's hair dryer.

And if your tree falls on the ground,
he's lazy and his roots aren't sound.
You've done the very best you could.
Now chop him up for firewood.

ALLAN WOLF

How to Make a Snow Angel

Go alone or with a best friend.
Find a patch of unbroken snow.

Walk on tiptoes. Step backwards
Into your very last footprints.

Slowly sit back onto the snow.
Absolutely do not use your hands.

By now you should be lying flat
With snow fitting snug around you.

Let your eyes drink some blue sky.
Close them. Breathe normally.

Move your arms back and forth.
Concentrate. Think: snow angel.

In a minute don't be surprised
If you start feeling a little funny.

Big and small. Warm and cold.
Your breath light as a snowflake.

Sweep your legs back and forth
But keep your eyes tightly closed.

Keep moving the arms until they
Lift, tremble, wobble, or float.

Stand without using your hands.
Take time to get your balance.

Take three deep breaths.
Open your eyes.

Stretch. Float. Fly!

RALPH FLETCHER

How to Be a Snowflake

Fashion yourself:
a bit of lace,
crystalline,
spun in space
of silken ice,
silvery, fine —
YOU create
your own design.

ELAINE MAGLIARO

Snowflake Catcher

Remove gloves,

Elevate palms

To chest level,

Face them toward

Vaulted ceiling,

Let frosted filigree

Settle into your paws

Melting its signature

Into yours.

CHARLES WATERS

On the Fourth of July

Take one dark sky,

Mix one large crowd,

   prepared beforehand to be quite loud.

Set rockets down,

Wait for cues.

   Now it's time to light a fuse.

There it goes — there's the first.

Watch it rise, watch it burst.

   Gold to red, red to blue.

Fireworks! Let's all go, "Oooh!"

MARILYN SINGER

Fireworks

Snuggle close
Mommy's hands cover my ears
Boom-ba-da-boom

Is it over?

Silver worms
Whistling in the night
Clouds of fairies
Crackle and pop

Is it over?

Raining gumdrops
Falling berries

Can we do it again?

ANNA E. JORDAN

Tired Hair

If you're tired of your hair,
Rope it to a rocking chair.

Hang it from a chandelier;
Wrap it round a fishing pier.

Tie it into fifty knots;
Dye it green with purple spots.

Hitch it to a railroad train;
Stitch it with your middle name.

Mail it first class in a letter;
Weave it in your cashmere sweater.

Comb it with a garden rake;
Mix it in a chocolate cake.

Feed it to a hungry pig;
Then go out and buy a wig.

DOUGLAS FLORIAN

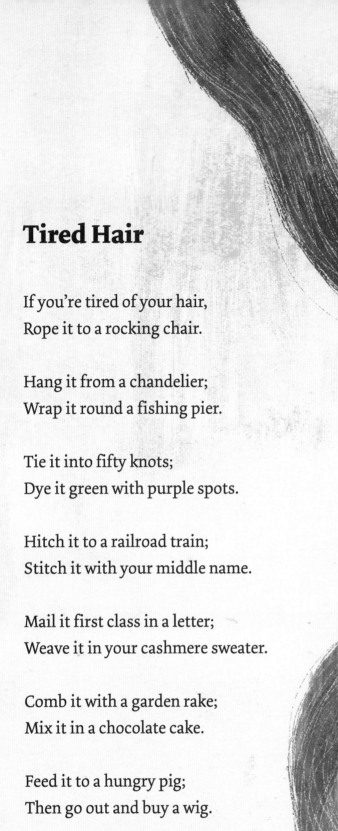

Barbershop

When you visit the barber
    And sit in his chair,
Don't squirm
Like a worm
    While he's cutting your hair.

Don't shiver
And quiver
    And bounce up and down.
Don't shuffle
And snuffle
    And act like a clown.

Each wiggle
Will jiggle
    The blades of the shears.
Clip-clip,
Clip-clip.
Those scissors can slip
And snip
Off a tip
    Of one of your tender pink ears!

MARTIN GARDNER

A Lesson from the Deaf

First, sweep one hand
up to your mouth,
as if to blow a velvet kiss.
Like this.

Second, drop that hand
into the other,
crisscross, open palms staring
at the sky.
Do you see?
How your clever hands
create a butterfly?

(Think of shadows
you shape upon a wall at night.
But this is more than play.)

Stand before someone
who has been kind to you.
Follow steps one and two,
and without breathing a word,
your "thank you" will be heard.

NIKKI GRIMES

How to Read Braille

Sail your fingerships
Over a paper sea
You cannot see

Sail your fingerships
Across a dotted alphabet
Shaped like wave caps

Forward and back
And do not stop
Until you touch bottom

Of the great, wide page.

STEVEN WITHROW

Best Friends

To call across a summer night
and tell your friend,
I'm over here. Let's meet!
look for a whistle
in the grass at your feet.
Pick a blade of crabgrass
flat and wide.
Hold your thumbs
like best friends
standing side by side.
With the grass
between your thumbs—
hold it straight and tight—
bring grass and thumbs
up to your mouth
and blow. It might
take a try or two.
Keep trying
till your friend hears
your grass-whistle
and comes to stand by you.

HELEN FROST

How to Say a Little Prayer

Choose a place you like,
a bright, sunny space,
or by the sea rippling—in and out—
or a hilltop, or your bed at night.

Slowly, breathe in and out, in and out.

Think about a sight you like—
yellow flowers, your mom's face,
a favorite tree, a hawk in flight—
breathing slowly in and out.

Think about a memory that makes you smile—
breathing in and out—
a good-night kiss or Granddad patting your head
then hugging you so tight.

Eyes closed, still breathing slowly,
whisper, "*Gracias*, thanks."

A little prayer for our many blessings
        feels right.

PAT MORA

How to Catch a Poem

Step into the trees
on a summer night —

follow starshine
and cricketsong.

Be still, keep quiet;
watch for the flicker.

(No chasing,
let it come to you.)

Reach. Hold it in the safe
cave of your fingers

until the wings tickle.
Marvel at the glow

           then

let it go.

IRENE LATHAM

How to Pay Attention

Close this book.
Look.

April Halprin Wayland

Acknowledgments

"How to Build a Poem" by Charles Ghigna. Copyright © 2016 by Charles Ghigna. Used with permission of the author.

"How to Tell a Camel" by J. Patrick Lewis. Copyright © 1990 by J. Patrick Lewis. Reprinted by permission of Curtis Brown, Ltd.

"How to Be a Mole" and "How to Be a Snowflake" by Elaine Magliaro. Used by permission of Elaine Magliaro.

"The Proper Way to Meet a Hedgehog" and "How to Take Care of Your Tree" by Allan Wolf. Used by permission of Allan Wolf.

"Toasting Marshmallows" and "On the Fourth of July" by Marilyn Singer. Copyright © by Marilyn Singer. "Toasting Marshmallows" originally published in *Central Heating* (Knopf, 2005).

"To Make a Meal" by Calef Brown. Copyright © 2015 by Calef Brown.

"How to Tell Goblins from Elves" from *Goose Grass Rhymes* by Monica Shannon, copyright 1930 by Doubleday, an imprint of Random House Children's Books. Copyright © renewed 1957 by Monica Shannon Wing. Used by permission of Doubleday, an imprint of the Knopf Doubleday Publishing Group, a division of Penguin Random House LLC. All rights reserved.

"How to Scare Monsters" by Rebecca Kai Dotlich. Copyright © 2017 by Rebecca Kai Dotlich. Used by permission of Curtis Brown, Ltd.

"Rules" by Karla Kuskin. Copyright © 1962, renewed 1980 by Karla Kuskin. Used by permission of S©ott Treimel NY.

"Rules of Speaking" and "Tired Hair" by Douglas Florian. Used by permission of Douglas Florian.

"Walking on Mars," "How to Be a Tree in Winter," and "How to Catch a Poem" by Irene Latham. Used by permission of Irene Latham.

"Table Tennis Triolet" by Marjorie Maddox. First appeared in *And the Crowd Goes Wild! A Global Gathering of Sports Poems*, edited by Carol-Ann Hoyte and Heidi Bee Roemer.

"Basketball Rule #2" from *The Crossover* by Kwame Alexander. Copyright © 2014 by Kwame Alexander. Reprinted by permission of Houghton Mifflin Harcourt Publishing Company. All rights reserved.

"How to Ride a New Bike" and "How to Pay Attention" by April Halprin Wayland. Copyright © 2016 by April Halprin Wayland. Used by permission of the author, who controls all rights.

"Playin' Jacks" and "Fireworks" by Anna E. Jordan. Copyright © 2004 by Anna E. Jordan. Reprinted with the permission of the poet.

"How to Bird-Watch" by Margarita Engle. Used by permission of Margarita Engle.

PAUL B. JANECZKO (1945–2019) was a poet and teacher who edited numerous award-winning poetry anthologies for young people, including *A Poke in the I*, *A Kick in the Head*, *A Foot in the Mouth*, and *The Death of the Hat*, all of which were illustrated by Chris Raschka, as well as *Firefly July*, illustrated by Melissa Sweet.

RICHARD JONES has worked for more than twenty years in the creative arts. He is the illustrator of numerous picture books, including *Bird Builds a Nest* and *The Squirrels' Busy Year*, both by Martin Jenkins. He lives in Devon, England.

In memoriam
Holly Fenn

For Jim Schneider —
poet, storyteller, friend
"Every good story is worth repeating."
P. B. J.

For Zara
R. J.

Compilation copyright © 2019 by Paul B. Janeczko
Illustrations copyright © 2019 by Richard Jones
Copyright acknowledgments appear on page 46

First edition 2019

Library of Congress Catalog Card Number 2018961359
ISBN 978-0-7636-8168-5

19 20 21 22 23 CCP 10 9 8 7 6 5 4 3 2

Printed in Shenzhen, Guangdong, China

This book was typeset in Dolly.
The illustrations were rendered in paint and edited digitally.

Candlewick Press
99 Dover Street
Somerville, Massachusetts 02144

visit us at www.candlewick.com